Socrates
Greek Philosopher

Lisa Zamosky

Publishing Credits

Content Consultant
Blane Conklin, Ph.D.

Associate Editor
Christina Hill, M.A.

Assistant Editor
Torrey Maloof

Editorial Assistants
Deborah Buchanan
Kathryn R. Kiley
Judy Tan

Editorial Director
Emily R. Smith, M.A.Ed.

Editor-in-Chief
Sharon Coan, M.S.Ed.

Editorial Manager
Gisela Lee, M.A.

Creative Director
Lee Aucoin

Cover Designer
Lesley Palmer

Designers
Deb Brown
Zac Calbert
Amy Couch
Robin Erickson
Neri Garcia

Publisher
Rachelle Cracchiolo, M.S.Ed.

Teacher Created Materials
5301 Oceanus Drive
Huntington Beach, CA 92649
http://www.tcmpub.com
ISBN 978-0-7439-0435-3

Table of Contents

Who Was Socrates?

Socrates (SAWK-ruh-teez) was an ancient Greek **philosopher** (fuh-LAWS-uh-fuhr). He helped to shape Greek beliefs. The ideas he created are present in our **culture** today.

Socrates was born in 470 B.C. He grew up during the Golden Age of Athens. This was a time period when Greece was very powerful. His family lived near Athens.

▼ The Acropolis was built during the Golden Age of Athens.

Map of ancient Greece

When Socrates was young, his father wanted him to become a sculptor. Once he was old enough, he worked with his father. He learned how to cut and shape stone.

Greek Geography

Greece is located on the southern tip of Europe. It borders the Aegean (ih-JEE-uhn), Adriatic (ay-dree-AT-ik), and Mediterranean (MED-uh-tuhr-RAY-nee-uhn) seas. Greece is made up of a large mainland surrounded by many smaller islands.

Greece Is Growing

The Minoans (muh-NO-uhnz) were the first great **civilization** (siv-uh-luh-ZAY-shuhn) of the ancient Greek world. Then, the Mycenaean (my-suh-NEE-uhn) people arrived around 1600 B.C. Around the eighth century B.C., Greek towns began to grow.

What We Know

Socrates never wrote anything about his own life. Other people wrote everything known about him. For this reason, we do not know much about his early life.

Two men who wrote about Socrates were Plato and Xenophon (ZEN-uh-fuhn). Both these men were students of Socrates. Like Socrates, Plato was a philosopher. Plato included his own ideas with Socrates's ideas. Xenophon was a soldier and a farmer. His stories describe Socrates as a good person and teacher.

Aristotle (AIR-uh-stawt-uhl) was another philosopher. He was Plato's student. Aristotle also wrote about Socrates. His writings seem to give a fair account of Socrates. But, Aristotle never actually knew Socrates.

▲ Plato was Aristotle's teacher.

Xenophon's writings describe Socrates for people today.

Zeus was king of the gods.

Plato or Socrates?

Plato recorded conversations Socrates had with people. These **dialogues** (DIE-uh-logs) are now classics of world literature. People today are not sure which thoughts are Plato's ideas and which are Socrates's ideas.

The Clouds

Aristophanes (air-uh-STAWF-uh-neez) wrote a comic play called *The Clouds*. This play makes fun of Socrates. The play shows a lot about Socrates's life as a young philosopher. The play is still performed today in theaters around the world.

Greek Myths

The Greeks believed that the gods controlled every part of their lives. Greek myths are stories about these gods. Legends include human heroes with the gods. There are many different versions of these stories. Greek mythology is still studied and enjoyed.

Life in Athens

When Socrates was young, Greece fought the Persian (PURR-zhuhn) War. The Persian Empire attacked Athens in 492 B.C. The huge Persian army outnumbered the Greeks. Even so, after many years of fighting, the Greeks won the war. This victory began the Golden Age of Athens.

During the Golden Age, a man named Pericles (PER-uh-kleez) led Athens. He wanted to make Athens a great city. Athens welcomed artists, scientists, and musicians. Beautiful temples and sculptures were created during this time. Great plays and poems were written. The creations of this period had an impact on the world for centuries to come.

The Parthenon ▼ in Athens

▲ Greek plays were performed in outdoor theaters.

All types of science interested the Greeks. They made many advances in biology, mathematics, astronomy, and geography. An important area of Greek science was medicine. The Greeks developed treatments for many diseases.

Pericles was a strong ruler. ▶

Great Plays

Both Sophocles (SAWF-uh-kleez) and Euripides (you-RIP-uh-deez) wrote plays during the Golden Age of Athens. These plays are still performed in theaters all around the world.

Women in Athens

In ancient Greece, men controlled the lives of women. The world outside the home was mostly off-limits to women. They were not allowed to participate in public life. Women could only leave the house for very special events.

Acropolis

The word *acropolis* (uh-KRAWP-uh-luhs) means "high city" in Greek. The Acropolis in Athens was built as a religious center of the city. It was also a place where the citizens could hide when enemies attacked. The Parthenon (PAR-thuh-nawn) is a large temple on the Acropolis. It was built to honor the goddess Athena.

This image shows some of the best-known Greek philosophers.

Curious Socrates

From the time Socrates was a young man, he searched for wisdom and truth. He gained wisdom by asking questions. Many people in Athens thought that they had answers. Socrates asked them questions. He argued with them about different topics. He did not think they had the knowledge they claimed to have.

During this time, there was a group of people called Sophists (SAWF-istz) in Athens. Sophists were paid to lecture and teach people.

Spartan soldier

They taught men how to speak well and influence others. But, they also used their abilities to cheat people out of money. Many people thought that Socrates was a Sophist because of the way he spoke. But, he was not a Sophist.

Sparta

Sparta was a **city-state** at the same time as Athens. Life in Sparta was very different from life in Athens. Sparta was a city that was led by military leaders. In Sparta, people had to be disciplined and loyal. These were the traits most valued in a person.

Building New Ideas

Socrates challenged false ideas people had about things like justice, love, or courage. He would break down the ideas people held. Then, he built new, more accurate ideas. Socrates felt that this was what philosophy was all about. Since then, great philosophers have used this method to find the truth.

Diogenes (di-AWJ-uh-neez) was a well-known Sophist.

Work for Free

Throughout his life, Socrates showed no interest in money. He was also not interested in material items. Socrates would allow groups of men to listen to him speak. And, he would never take money from them. He always wore the same clothes, no matter the season.

Socrates argued that his life was better because he had no material wealth. He felt that he enjoyed his food more. He said that he was stronger and healthier because he was not affected by the weather. Socrates said that happiness came not from having more but from wanting less.

Greek Slaves

In ancient Greece, slaves were a very important part of society. Wealthy women did not leave their homes. So, their slaves took care of everyday household chores. Shopping, getting water, and buying food were jobs for slaves.

The Republic

Plato wrote a set of ten books about justice. The books were called the *Republic*. Plato's *Republic* is carefully studied around the world today.

Taking a Stand

Socrates would stand on a *stoa* (STOH-uh), or platform, while teaching others. Ruins of stone *stoas* can still be seen in Athens today.

◀ Socrates often wore ragged clothing.

This is a rebuilt stone *stoa* in Athens. ▶

Strange Behavior

Socrates was known for being a bit strange. He went into a **trance** when he thought hard about a problem. He might stand still for days on end without moving, eating, or sleeping. Men in the city would gather around Socrates to watch him. Once he was finished thinking, he would snap out of his trance and go on as usual.

Socrates also claimed to have an inner voice that spoke to him. This voice would guide him when he needed help deciding what

Socrates is remembered with many beautiful statues.

to do. His voice told him whether or not something was a good idea. People often told Socrates to get involved in politics. His inner voice always advised him against it.

Wise Through the Years

Many of Socrates's observations have been commonly repeated over thousands of years. Some of his observations are still followed today.

"False words are not only evil in themselves, but they infect the soul with evil."

"Let him that would move the world first move himself."

"We are what we repeatedly do. Excellence, then, is a habit."

"Wisdom begins in wonder."

▼ This famous Italian painting is called *The School of Athens*. Many famous Greeks are shown.

This map shows Greece during the Peloponnesian War.

Socrates as a Soldier

When Socrates was 40 years old, another war broke out in Athens. The Greek city-states of Athens and Sparta fought in the Peloponnesian (pel-uh-puhn-NEE-zhuhn) War. They both wanted to control Greece.

Socrates served as a **hoplite** (HAWP-lite). Hoplites were the foot soldiers of the Greek army. These men brought their own **armor** to battle. This means that hoplites had to have enough money to buy the armor they needed to fight. Socrates bought his armor, too. He may not have been as poor as he wanted people to think.

▲ Modern marathons are still about 26 miles.

Socrates fought for three years and then returned to Athens. Normally, he denied himself food and warm clothing. So, being a soldier may not have been as hard for him as it was for others.

Alexander the Great ▶

The First Marathon

Remember the Persian War earlier in Socrates's life? There is a famous story about that war. A Greek man ran about 26 miles (about 42 km) to announce that Athens had beaten the Persians. He ran without stopping from the battlefield at Marathon to Athens. Because of this legend, a 26.2-mile marathon was run at the Olympic games in 1896. Marathons are still run today.

Alexander the Great

The most famous Greek soldier was Alexander the Great. He was a very powerful leader. The men in the army would do anything for him. Alexander wanted to create the largest empire in the world. By his death, his empire stretched from Greece to northern India.

Apollo's Gift

The gods were very important to the people in ancient Greece. Poseidon (puh-SY-duhn) was the god of the seas and rivers. Aphrodite (ahf-ruh-DIE-tee) was the goddess of love and beauty. Athena (uh-THEE-nuh) was the protector of Athens. And, Apollo (uh-PAWL-lo) controlled the sun and light. The god Apollo was the most important god to Socrates.

Socrates believed that his job was to gain wisdom by asking questions. He spent his days walking the streets of Athens talking to people. He spoke with men from all walks of life. Musicians, athletes, poets, and merchants were all interesting to Socrates. Socrates was very well-known in Athens, but not everyone liked him. Crowds would often gather to listen to Socrates. He would embarrass people with his questions. The men who were defeated by his arguments often

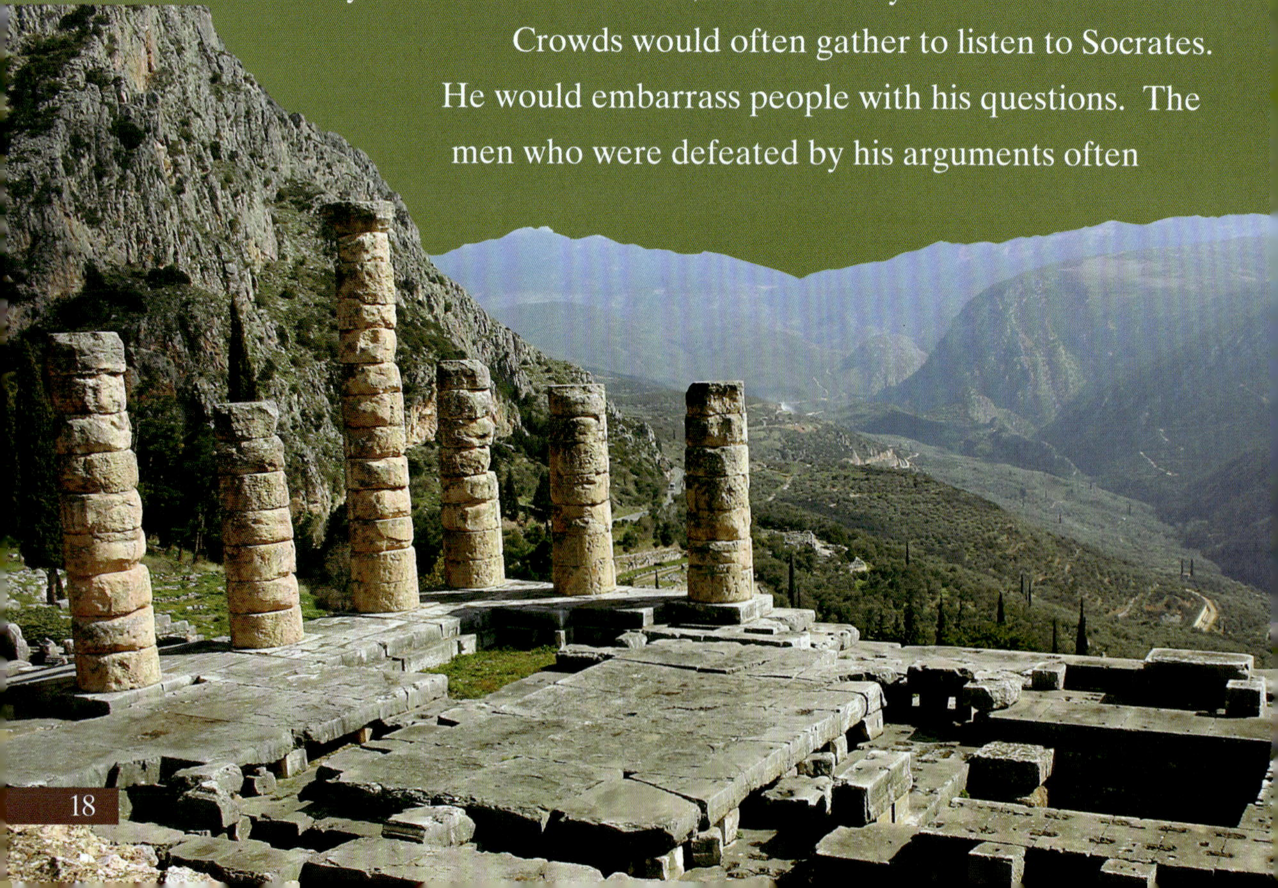

▲ The modern Greek military is still strong.

disliked him. Others admired Socrates for his skill. He could beat anyone in an argument. Many men wanted to learn how to argue and reason just like Socrates.

Military Power

Ancient Greek military power was among the strongest in history. Even today, all healthy Greek citizens between the ages of 18 and 60 must be ready for military service.

Apollo at Delphi

Temples were built to honor the gods. Apollo was worshipped in the town of Delphi (DEL-fie). He spoke to people through a priestess. She was at the temple of Apollo. The temple of Apollo was built with donations from all the city-states and some foreign countries. The temple today still has six of its original columns.

◀ Ruins of the Temple of Apollo at Delphi

◀ Greeks believed that Poseidon controlled the seas.

Genuine Self-Knowledge

When he talked to people, Socrates liked to ask questions. He did not have certain answers that he wanted. He just wanted to find the truth. Socrates spent a lot of time revealing false beliefs that people held.

He used this method to teach his students. Socrates did not teach anything specific. He wanted students to learn how to decide what they truly believed. To do this, they needed to understand their own feelings and beliefs. That is why he asked so many questions.

▼ Socrates questioning his students

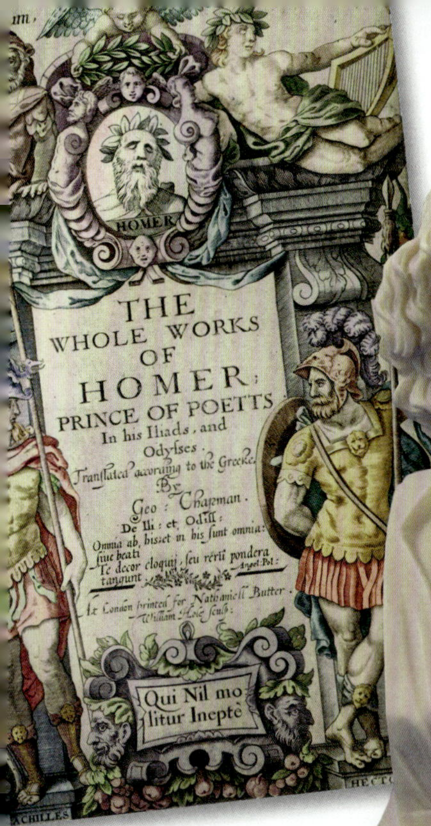

Homer ▶

This method of asking questions is called the Socratic (suh-KRAT-ik) Method. Its goal is to help people find truth. It is important that people know the truth, even if it is negative. Socrates thought that questioning was the only way to become a true philosopher.

Greek Literature

Homer was a Greek poet. In Greek schools, teachers used Homer's writings. His two epic poems were the *Iliad* (IL-ee-uhd) and the *Odyssey* (AWD-uh-see). These long poems were used to teach young Greek boys how to read.

Socrates and the Law

The Socratic Method is very important in modern-day law schools. This method is used to start classroom discussions about laws. When a teacher asks many questions, students are able to think through a problem. Answering questions lets students study their own beliefs more closely. They might even realize that their beliefs are false.

Socrates on Trial

By the end of the fifth century B.C., Athens was not a great city anymore. **Politicians** (pawl-uh-TIH-shuhnz) betrayed Athens. And, many young men had died in the wars. A **plague** (PLAYG) killed a huge number of Athenians.

Socrates had made many people angry over the years. He had been very critical of laws and policies. Athens had a new group of political

▼ This shows Pericles's funeral. He died of the plague.

Plato and Socrates worked closely together.

leaders in power. They did not want to hear Socrates's comments about them.

Many people thought that Socrates was a bad influence on the young people of Athens. He was also accused of not **worshipping** the right gods. Charges were brought against him. The politicians wanted the death penalty for Socrates.

Discussing Democracy

In one of Plato's books, Socrates and another Greek discuss **democracy**. The two men talk about whether or not a common man is good enough to be a leader. This document holds many ideas about democracy that are still important today.

Influencing the Romans

Because of Alexander the Great, Greek influence was felt all over the world. The Romans had similar gods. Their plays were based on Greek stories. And, even the Roman government had ties back to Greek democracy.

GET OUT OF ATHENS

Socrates's friends told him to leave Athens. They thought this was the only way for him to save his life. Socrates refused. He did not behave as most people in his situation would. Socrates said that he had always lived by the rules of Athens and he would continue to do this. He insisted on standing **trial** for his "crimes."

◀ Socrates defends himself at his trial.

Socrates knew he was not guilty of anything. The reason he was being charged was because he was different from others. Although people respected Socrates, he also made many people angry. During his trial he spoke in his own defense. In the end he would not beg for his life. The jury said Socrates was guilty.

▲ Courtrooms today are very different than they were in ancient Greece.

The Apology

Plato wrote about Socrates's statements at his trial. The book is called *The Apology*. In this case, an *apology* means a "defense." This document is read today to study Socrates.

Famous Saying

Socrates was fond of saying "All I know is that I know nothing." Many people in modern times have used Socrates's words to reflect their own feelings about knowledge and wisdom.

Democracy's Birthplace

Socrates was put on trial. This was part of the democratic system of government set up by the Greeks. Athens is considered the birthplace of democracy. Many governments around the world today, including the United States, are democracies.

Execution

When faced with the death penalty, a person could leave Athens forever. This would be instead of being put to death. Most people chose to leave rather than die. Socrates was not like most people.

Instead of telling the jury that he would go, he told them that he deserved a reward. Socrates believed that he had done a great service by making people think. Socrates said that he tried to "persuade every one

▼ Socrates was given hemlock in jail.

of you not to think of what he had but rather of what he was, and how he might grow wise and good."

The jury did not change its mind. Socrates was **executed** (EKS-ih-kyoot-ed). He died when he drank **hemlock**, which is poisonous.

Friedrich Nietzsche

Fellow Philosopher

Not everyone in history had a high opinion of Socrates. German philosopher Friedrich Nietzsche (FREE-drik NEE-chee) called Socrates "the buffoon who got himself taken seriously."

Singing Until the End

While in his jail cell, Socrates set some of Aesop's (EH-sawpz) Fables to music. These fables are classics of literature.

Socrates's Contribution

Dr. King speaks in Washington, D.C.

Socrates was the first great Greek philosopher. His ideas continue to influence society today. He asked questions and argued with people to find the truth. Socrates wanted to expose things and people for what they really were. This was more important to him than anything else.

Socrates helped to shape other philosophers that came after him. Plato and Aristotle also changed Western civilization. Plato got his start by studying with Socrates. And, then Aristotle studied with Plato.

Asking questions to discover the truth is still practiced today. Schools teach this method to students. Socrates's impact on civilization has been felt for over 2,000 years.

Martin Luther King Jr.

Dr. Martin Luther King took inspiration from Socrates while he was in jail. In 1963, he wrote a famous letter from a jail in Birmingham, Alabama. In his letter he spoke about tension. He said that he agreed with Socrates. It is necessary to create tension in order to "rise from the bondage of myths and half-truths."

Influence in India

Socrates also inspired Mohandas Gandhi (mo-HAWN-duhs GAWN-dee). Gandhi lived in India. Socrates was not very handsome. Gandhi said that despite his looks, Socrates was a beautiful person because he spent his life searching for truth.

Mohandas Gandhi

Glossary

armor—a protective cover of metal, wood, or leather

city-state—an ancient city that ruled itself independently

civilization—society that has writing and keeps track of records

culture—people's way of life, including art, religion, music, and language.

democracy—government that is ruled by the people

dialogues—conversations between people

executed—put to death

hemlock—poison

hoplite—a foot soldier in the ancient Greek army

philosopher—a student of philosophy, which is thinking based on reason

plague—a widespread disease

politicians—people who serve in a government

trance—a state that is between sleeping and being awake

trial—examining evidence and laws to decide about a charge that has been made

worshipping—honoring with great respect

Index

Image Credits

cover Hulton Archive/Getty Images; p.1 Hulton Archive/Getty Images; p.4 Lysippos/The Bridgeman Art Library/Getty Images; pp.4–5 Nick Koumaris/Shutterstock, Inc.; p.5 (top) The Historical Atlas by William R. Shepherd, 1923; p.6 Raphael/The Bridgeman Art Library/Getty Images; p.7 (top) Classic Image/Alamy; p.7 (bottom) Photos.com; p.8 Clement K.L. Cheah/Shutterstock, Inc.; p.9 (top) Styve Reineck/Shutterstock, Inc.; p.9 (bottom) The Granger Collection, New York; p.10 The Granger Collection, New York; p.11 (top) The Granger Collection, New York; p.11 (bottom) The Granger Collection, New York; p.12 Teacher Created Materials; p.13 Adam Carr; p.14 Andreas Guskos/Shutterstock, Inc.; p.15 SuperStock, Inc.; p.16 The Historical Atlas by William R. Shepherd, 1923; p.17 (top) Byron W. Moore/Shutterstock, Inc.; p.17 (bottom) Vladimir Korostyshevskiy/Shutterstock, Inc.; p.18 Mike Liu/Shutterstock, Inc.; p.19 (top) iStockphoto/Szymon Mazurek; p.19 (bottom) Stephen St John/National Geographic/Getty Images; p.20 The Granger Collection, New York; p.21 (top left) Mary Evans Picture Library/Alamy; p.21 (top right) Barry G Hurt/Shutterstock, Inc.; p.21 (bottom) Erick Jones/Shutterstock, Inc.; p.22 The Granger Collection, New York; p.23 The Granger Collection, New York; p.24 Mary Evans Picture Library/Alamy; p.25 Ron Chapple/Getty Images; pp.26–27 The Granger Collection, New York; p.27 Hulton Archive/Getty Images; p.28 Photos.com; p.29 (top) National Archives and Records Administration; p.29 (bottom) Arteki/Shutterstock, Inc.; back cover Andreas Guskos/Shutterstock, Inc.